I Love Ponies...

Learn to Ride

Sandy Ransford

QEB Publishing

Editor: Amanda Askew
Designer: Izzy Langridge

Copyright © QEB Publishing, Inc. 2011

First published in the United States in 2011 by
QEB Publishing, Inc.
3 Wrigley, Suite A
Irvine, CA 92618

www.qed-publishing.co.uk

Library of Congress Cataloging-in-Publication Data

Ransford, Sandy.
 Learn to ride / Sandy Ransford.
    p. cm. -- (I love ponies)
 Includes index.
 Summary: "Covers all the basics of horse riding, from mounting and
dismounting to saddle positions, holding the reins, and trotting, cantering,
and galloping"--Provided by publisher.
 ISBN 978-1-60992-100-2 (library bound)
 1. Horsemanship--Juvenile literature. 2. Horses--Juvenile literature. I.
Title. II. Series.

SF309.2.R37 2012
636.1--dc22

                         2011009129

ISBN 978 1 60992 100 2

Printed in China

Picture credits
(t=top, b=bottom, l=left, r=right, c=center, fc=front cover)
All images are courtesy of Bob Langrish images unless stated below.
Dreamstime fc, 1 Asso59
DK Images 4bl, 4br Kit Houghton, 7t Dorling Kindersley, 7bl David
Handley, 8 Kit Houghton, 11t Dorling Kindersley
Shutterstock 1b Peter Baxter, 2bl Jeff Banke, 10 Tamara Didenko, 11t
Tihis, 20 Groomee

Words in **bold** are explained in the glossary on page 22.

Remember!
Children must always
wear appropriate clothing,
including a riding hat, and
follow safety guidelines
when handling or riding
horses and ponies.

Contents

Mounting and Dismounting

Mounting means getting on a pony and dismounting means getting off it. To help you get on the pony, you can use a mounting block or someone can give you a **leg up**—but you also need to be able to do it without help.

Using a Mounting Block

Standing on a block helps when the pony is tall or if you don't have much bounce. It also prevents you from pulling the saddle over as you spring up.

Getting a Leg Up

To get a leg up, first ask someone to hold the lower part of your left leg. Then when you're ready, they can push you up as you spring off your right foot.

1

2

3

4

5

Dismounting

To dismount safely, take both feet out of the stirrups. Lean forward to the pony's left side, and swing your right leg over the saddle and the pony's **quarters**. Take care not to catch it with your toe, and slide to the ground, landing on both feet.

Mounting Without Help

1. Stand on the pony's left side, facing its tail. Hold the **reins** in your left hand.

2. Put your left foot in the **stirrup iron**.

3. Spring up off your right foot, take hold of the saddle with your right hand, and swing your right leg over the saddle.

4. Sit down gently.

5. Turn the front of the right stirrup iron outwards and slip in your right foot.

In the Saddle

When you first sit on a pony, it may feel strange. Try to relax and sit comfortably. Keep your back straight and allow your legs to hang down naturally. Your stirrups will be around the right length if the bottom of the iron is level with your instep.

Top Tip!
Before you set off, ask someone to check the **girth** is tight enough.

Adjusting the Stirrups

You can adjust the length of the stirrups by pulling up the end of the leather and sliding the buckle up or down. Make sure the prong is in the hole. Pull down the underside of the leather so the buckle is under the buckle guard.

At first, you may need help to find the stirrup with your right foot.

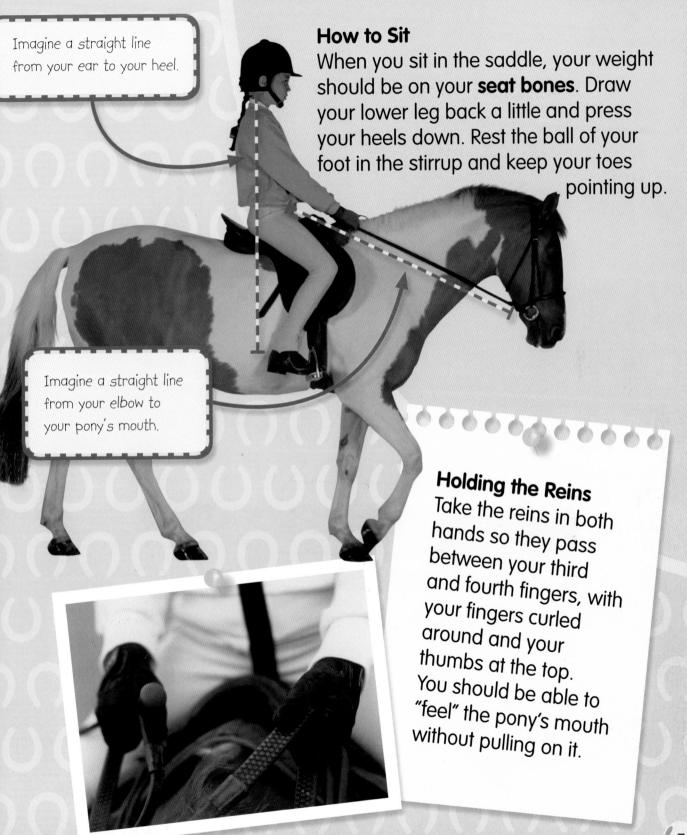

Imagine a straight line from your ear to your heel.

How to Sit

When you sit in the saddle, your weight should be on your **seat bones**. Draw your lower leg back a little and press your heels down. Rest the ball of your foot in the stirrup and keep your toes pointing up.

Imagine a straight line from your elbow to your pony's mouth.

Holding the Reins

Take the reins in both hands so they pass between your third and fourth fingers, with your fingers curled around and your thumbs at the top. You should be able to "feel" the pony's mouth without pulling on it.

Riding at Walk

To tell a horse or pony what to do, you use signals called "**aids**." You give these signals with your legs, hands, seat, body weight, and voice. These are called "natural aids." Experienced riders can also give signals with whips and spurs—these are called "artificial aids."

Keep contact with the pony's mouth with the reins, but don't hold your arms and hands stiffly.

Walking Forward

To tell a pony to walk forward, shorten your reins a little and press your lower legs into its sides. You can also say "Walk on" in an encouraging tone of voice. As soon as the pony moves forward, ease the pressure with your legs, but keep in contact with the pony's sides. Allow your hands to follow the movement of the pony's head.

Tapping a pony on the quarters with a long schooling whip will tell it to move its back legs over.

Spurs are fitted over riding boots. When they are used correctly, they can make a horse or pony carry out actions with only the slightest pressure.

How to Halt
To stop, press your legs into the pony's sides, but hold the reins firmly so it cannot move forward. You can also say "Whoa." When the pony has halted, release the pressure from your legs and hands and give it a pat on the neck and say "Good pony."

Learning to Trot

Trotting can be tricky, but it will become much easier with plenty of practice. Soon, you will be able to do it without thinking!

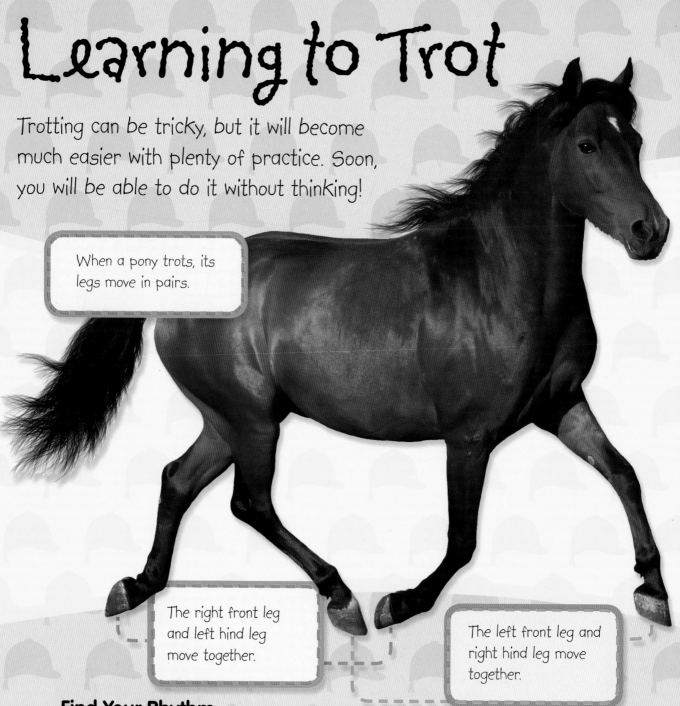

When a pony trots, its legs move in pairs.

The right front leg and left hind leg move together.

The left front leg and right hind leg move together.

Find Your Rhythm

Riding in trot can feel very bumpy. To make it more comfortable, rise up out of the saddle as one pair of the pony's feet hit the ground, and sit down as the opposite pair hit the ground.

Rising to the Trot

It is easier to practice **rising to the trot** with your pony standing still. Stand up in your stirrups and then sit down again gently.

Make sure not to thump down heavily— this will hurt your pony's back.

It's difficult to balance when you first learn to ride. You can try holding on to the saddle for extra support.

Top Tip!

Try to relax and allow your body to follow the motion of the pony.

Canter On

When a pony canters, its front and back legs on one side are in front of those on the other. So we say it is "leading" with the right or left leg. If you canter in a circle, or around a corner, the **leading leg** should be on the inside of the curve.

Preparing to Canter

Before you tell your pony to canter, you should be moving in a good, balanced trot. To canter with the right leg leading, shorten your reins and feel the right one more strongly than the left. Press with your right leg on the girth and with your left leg behind the girth.

This rider is sitting well and has her pony under control.

Into Canter

Once the pony goes into canter, relax the aids, but keep your reins fairly short. Because the pony's right leg is in front of its left, you will sit slightly askew, with your right shoulder slightly in front of your left shoulder. To canter with the left leg leading, reverse the aids.

1

2

3

4

Sitting to the Canter

The canter is a lovely, swinging pace, but at first you may bounce out of the saddle. Try to sit well down and allow your back relax to so you can follow the pony's movement. Avoid trying to hold yourself stiffly in position.

When you are cantering, you should be able to feel which leg the pony is leading with—without looking down.

These pictures show how the pony's feet hit the ground when it is cantering.

1. Most of its weight is on its right front leg.
2. Most of its weight is on its left hind leg.
3. Another stride begins with both front legs off the ground.
4. The weight is on the right front leg and left hind leg.

Top Tip!

If you lean forward when you are cantering, your pony will think you want it to go faster.

Turning your Pony

When a pony turns, its front legs and outer hind leg move around its inner hind leg. Its whole body curves, from head to tail.

Turning Right

When you turn a pony, your hand on the inside of the turn and your leg on the outside of the turn produce the movement.

1. Pull out the right rein to turn the pony's head to the right.

2. Move your left hand to the right, pressing the left rein against its neck.

3. At the same time, press with your left leg behind the girth to push the pony around.

4. Keep your right leg on the girth.

5. Both you and the pony should look in the direction in which you are going.

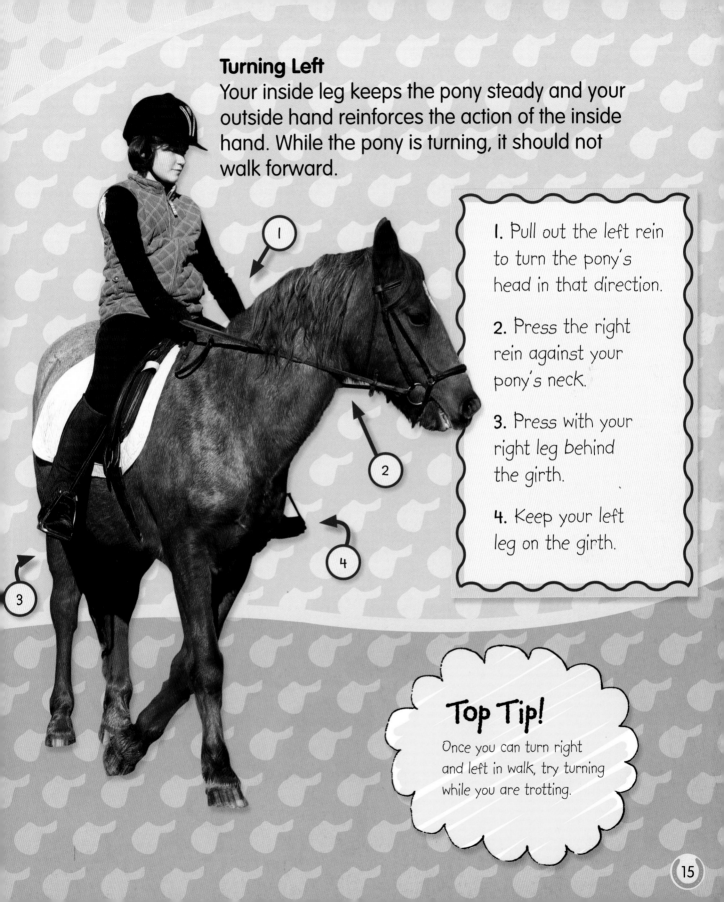

Turning Left

Your inside leg keeps the pony steady and your outside hand reinforces the action of the inside hand. While the pony is turning, it should not walk forward.

1. Pull out the left rein to turn the pony's head in that direction.

2. Press the right rein against your pony's neck.

3. Press with your right leg behind the girth.

4. Keep your left leg on the girth.

Top Tip!

Once you can turn right and left in walk, try turning while you are trotting.

Ride Western Style

Try riding Western style! First, your legs should be almost straight. Hold the reins in your right hand, separated by your first finger. Tell the pony to go forward by making a clucking sound, and to stop by saying "Whoa." When you trot in Western riding, sit down in the saddle instead of rising.

one-ear headstall

Western Bridle
This **bridle** has a loop in the **headstall** that fits around the pony's ear, and a curb **bit**. A bit is a metal bar that fits in the pony's mouth.

Saddle Up Fact!

Western bridles with bits do not usually have a noseband.

curb bit

Western Saddle

This saddle is much larger than an English one. The back part, called the cantle, is steeper. It has a horn at the front.

When cowboys are herding cattle, they can tie a cow to the horn with a rope. The stirrups are made of wood. This is more comfortable for the rider's feet than metal.

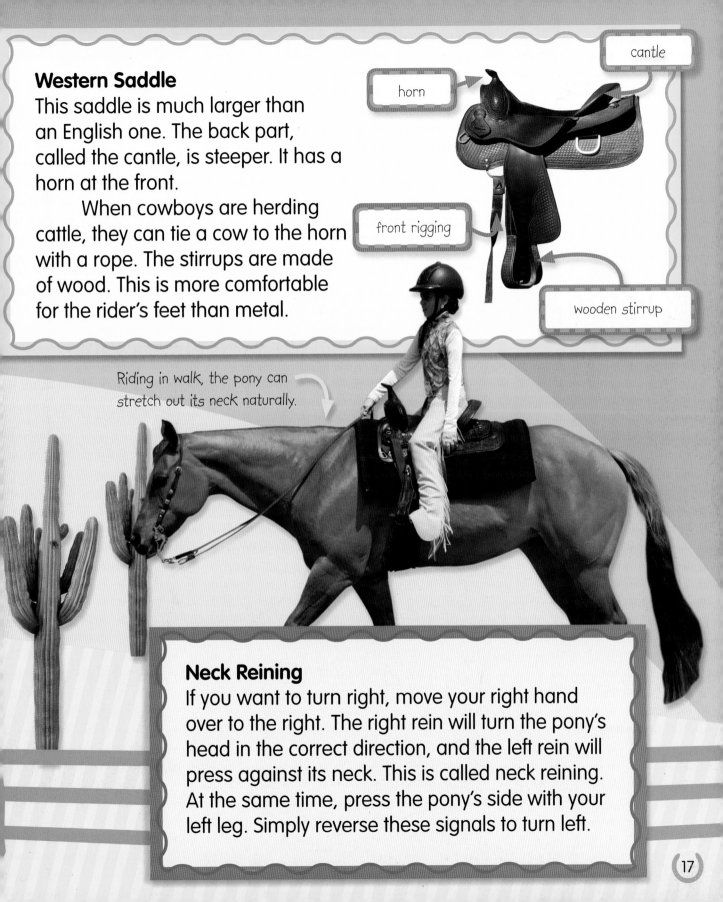

cantle

horn

front rigging

wooden stirrup

Riding in walk, the pony can stretch out its neck naturally.

Neck Reining

If you want to turn right, move your right hand over to the right. The right rein will turn the pony's head in the correct direction, and the left rein will press against its neck. This is called neck reining. At the same time, press the pony's side with your left leg. Simply reverse these signals to turn left.

Go for a Gallop

The gallop is the pony's fastest pace. Galloping is very exciting, both for the pony and its rider. Before you try to gallop, you must be able to control your pony in canter.

Saddle Up Fact!
A gallop is a four-beat gait. Each hoof hits the ground separately.

Forward Position
When you gallop, you take the weight off the pony's back by going into **"forward position"**— stand up slightly in your stirrups and lean forward. Practice going into forward position with the pony standing still and someone holding it.

Telling a Pony to Gallop

Start in a canter, then shorten your reins and go into forward position. Squeeze with both legs to urge the pony forward. As the pony goes faster, release the pressure from your legs but keep a firm hold of the reins. To slow down, press again with your legs and pull back strongly on the reins. Always allow plenty of space in which to stop.

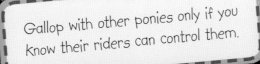

Gallop with other ponies only if you know their riders can control them.

Safety

You should gallop only where it is safe to do so—on a smooth, uphill track, free from stones and potholes. If you are with other ponies, allow plenty of space between them.

Learning to Jump

When you have learned to ride at walk, trot, and canter, you can try jumping. You need good balance in the saddle.

Trotting Rails

Your first lessons in learning to jump will be over **trotting rails**. These are rails on the ground, spaced so the pony can walk and trot over them. As you approach the rails, shorten your reins and go into forward position.

Your First Jump

As you approach the jump, shorten your reins and drive the pony forward with your legs. Go into forward position and sta[y] in that position until after the pon[y] has landed, so you don't pull on the reins and hurt its mouth.

When you are confident trotting over rails, you may take your first jump. This will not be very high.

Get Ready to Jump!

There are four stages to a jump.

1. The Approach

As you approach a jump, you will learn to "see the stride." This means judging how many strides the pony must take before it jumps so it can clear the rails.

2. Takeoff

As the pony takes off, it tucks up its front legs and springs off its hind legs. You must give with your hands to allow its neck to stretch forward.

3. In the Air

For a brief moment, all four legs are off the ground and the pony is "in the air."

4. Landing

The rider stays in forward position until the pony has landed. As it lands, the rider looks forwards to the next jump.

Glossary

Aids The signals you give your pony with your hands, legs, seat, body weight, and voice to tell it what you want it to do.

Bit A metal bar that goes in the pony's mouth. It is part of the bridle.

Bridle The headgear a pony wears when it is being ridden.

Forward position Leaning forward out of the saddle with your weight on the stirrups. This is used when you are galloping and jumping.

Girth The broad strap that goes around a pony's belly to hold the saddle in place.

Headstall The part of the bridle that fits over the top of the pony's head.

Leading leg The leg that is in front of the others when the pony is cantering.

Leg up An easy way of getting on a pony, when a helper holds your left leg and pushes you up into the saddle.

Quarters The back part of a pony—the hindquarters and hind legs.

Reins The parts of the bridle that attach to the bit. You hold the reins in your hands to control the pony.

Rising to the trot Standing up in stirrups as one pair of the pony's feet hits the ground, and then sitting down as the opposite pair of feet hits the ground.

Seat bones The bones that you sit on—in your backside.

Stirrup iron The metal loop in which you rest your foot when riding.

Trotting rails Rails laid on the ground, spaced so a pony can walk or trot over them.

Index

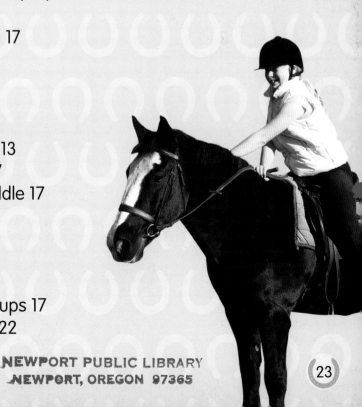

Notes for Parents and Teachers

- Ask children if they think it is extraordinary that an animal as large as a horse or pony can be controled by a child. Explain that the reason we can do this is because horses and ponies are herd animals that look to the dominant animal in the herd for leadership. When we handle them, we take the place of that dominant animal, and the pony expects to be told what to do.

- Explain that, for thousands of years, the horse was the only form of transport people had—apart from their own feet. Ask children if they have noticed that horses and ponies are many different sizes and shapes—why do they think this is and what do they think these different animals are used for? For example, compare a tall, lightly built racehorse, a large, heavily built draft horse, and a small riding pony.

- Horses and ponies are nervous animals, inclined to run away when anything startles them. Explain that this is because before they were domesticated, horses lived wild in herds and were hunted by predators, such as wolves. Discuss with children how we should handle horses and ponies, bearing this in mind, so as not to frighten them and to gain their trust (i.e. quietly and gently, without a lot of noise or fuss.)

- Explain that when riding or handling horses and ponies we have to feel confident. If we are nervous, the horse or pony may become nervous also, which can make them difficult to handle. If we handle them confidently, they feel safe and secure and will do as we tell them.